Adam and Cain

ΨΨΨΨΨΨΨΨΨΨΨΨΨΨΨΨΨΨΨΨΨ

by
Michael Graves

Cover Design and Illustrations
by
Robert J. Harding Jr.

December 17, '06

For Sybil,
Wide ranging and
powerful pret.
Michael Graves

BLACK BUZZARD PRESS

for William Rossky, James Wright,
Leonard Albert and Ellen Peckham

Published by Black Buzzard Press, a subsidiary of VIAS,
a nonprofit 501C3 arts organization

Acknowledgements: Some of these poems have appeared in the following publications, sometimes in slightly different form: Adam XV, XVI, XVII, and Cain's Agon with God as; III, IV as "You Who Create" and "Why Do You Hunger?" in NYCBigCityLit.com; Cain to Adam: I as "Cain's Desire" in Rattapallax, Cain to Eve: I as "You Ask Me How I've Been" in Magic Bullet, and "Cain at Abel's Grave" in The Sierra Mountain Review.

FIRST PRINTING, 2006

ISBN 0-938872-29-X

CONTENTS

ADAM

I. Satan Rises /1
II. I Went to the Tree /2
III. Cain, I Ate /3
IV. Beneath /4
V. Burdened /5
VI. Seraphs and Cherubs /6
VII. Eve, Eve /7
VIII. Kiss /8
IX. Your Mother and I /9
X. Rebuke /10
XI. Perhaps/ 11
XII. We Heard /12
XIII. Satan's Fool /13
XIV. Look at the Moon /14
XV. The Annihilating Glory /15
XVI. Come /16
XVII. Naked, I Went /17
XVIII. Why Should You Wonder? /18
XIX. Our Bones Will Listen /19
XX. Messenger /20
XXI. I Awakened Alone /21
XXII. Even in Terror /22
XXIII. There Was No Sin /23
XXIV. Banish the Rest /24
XXV. I Yearned for It /25

CAIN

Cain in Exile /26

Cain's Agon with God

I. The Wound /30
II. The Keeper /31
III. So I Intended /32

iii

IV. Who Was the First? /33
V. Why Do You Hunger? /34
VI. Confession and Question /35
VII. Reflection /37
VIII. Mark /38
IX. Goat /39
X. Refusal /40
XI. Will I Truly Be Safe? /41
XII. You Wonder at Murder? /42
XIII. Enough /43
XIV. Anguished, I Struggle /44
XV. Risen to Strike /45

Cain to Abel

I. Is It Not So? /46
II. Blest Is Your Peace /47
III. Provoke Me No Longer /48
IV. I Envy You Still /49

Cain to Adam

I. Like You, Adam /50
II. Tell Me Again /51
III. What Is Your Truth? /52
IV. Why Did You Spare Me? /53
V. Now That I Know /54
VI. As Fallen as You /55
VII. Think, Fool /56
VIII. I Will Return /57

Cain and Aklia

I. It Is Time /58

Cain Alone

I. O, Yes, I Will Offer /59
II. I Was Dismissed /60
III. I Dreamed of Their Words /61
IV. Song /62
V. You Rose from the Mud /63
VI. I Discarded My Crown /64
VII. Just Beyond the Bounds /65
VIII. Forgive Me My Favor /66
IX. I Shuddered and Woke /68

Cain to Eve

I. Beneath the Close, Mild Moon /69
II. In Dreams, I See Two Snaky Trees /70
III. Your Husband in His Sleep /72
IV. God Surely Would Die /73
V. You Saw You Were Second /74
VI. I Dreamed I Slid Among the Clothes /75
VII. "Like to the Father?" /76
VIII. Then, the Consoler in Heaven /77

Return

I. First of the Human /78
II. Like Smoke with the Sky /79

Beginnings are always earlier...

Thomas Mann

Water flows until it's purified,
And the weak bridegroom strengthens in the bride.

Theodore Roethke

Take away one vertebra and the two ends of this torturous
fantasy come together again without pain.

Charles Baudelaire

Adam and Cain

Adam

I

Satan rises
in the shape of a snake,
slithers out onto a limb,
with grief on his face.
Will he speak in praise of the
fruit?
In my dream he lay on the
floor
in front of the throne,
ready to strike,
disgusted by gold.
I open my eyes,
in love with his sorrow.

II

I went to the tree,
afraid of its dark, writhing
limbs,
but wanting to know…

That night,
I dreamed of a snake
that slept in the cleft trunk
as in the shrine of a God.
He draped your mother's
shape.
His head stroked her face.

In envy and terror
I shook awake.

III

Cain, I ate of it
long before your mother did,
and not because some
tempter spoke.

I feasted underneath the
limbs
of God's forbidden tree,
and then I slept
between two thick and
twisting roots.

IV

Beneath this storm-lit oak,
whose wind-ripped limbs
cast a net of shifting
shadows,
your eyes flash white.
Eve,
I hear you howl,
your hair as wild as
frightened snakes.
I have no reason
not to eat.

V

Burdened like goats,
we fell
in exhaustion and terror
in the wilderness
and struggled to act like
lovers,
not vipers.
From the first, Cain,
there was innocence, blessing
and filth.

VI

The seraphs and cherubs
staggered and reeled,
shielded their eyes
from the beams of my face,
murmured against me.
Jehovah dismissed them,
Cain,
with a wave
to kneel in the place where
you stand,
a place from which rocks and
snakes
have been cleared,
and I will raise an altar.

VII

Eve, Eve,
now the sun shines
like a flaming marriage torch,
and spring wind wakes!
The graceful Tree of Life
stretches and shivers
in the light!

VIII

I knelt
between your mother's
lifted legs
and bent my head to kiss.

Lifting off the guilty leaf,
I looked upon her hair.
It thinned and spread
like the branches
of the delicate forbidden
tree.

IX

Provoke you, Cain?
Can I avoid it?
Should I slither
with lips in the dirt
because you rage?
Before your birth
your mother and I fucked
earth
into blossom and harvest,
but you, afraid of your sex,
bring refuse to offer.

X

He interrupts.
He questions.
He seethes!
If he were silent,
there would be peace.
And you, you know the
danger.
The serpent in him
rises in us.
There will be violence...

XI

No.
You think I'd let your sullen
seed,
the poison of your loins,
infect my daughters?
Your children fill the earth?
Better none be born of any.
Love?
Love?
When angels sleep with
snakes,
then,
perhaps.

XII

Confession?
What could not be hidden
you call confession?
We heard the cry of Abel's
soul
scream in the heavens
and on the shaking earth.
You will say nothing,
except that you spoke
and went to the field
where you smashed at his
brains?

XIII

He's killed his brother!
And still he flings his cursing
threats!
He threatens you,
yet you, his easy loving
mother,
Satan's fool,
while Abel lies unburied,
beg me to forgive.
See how he scowls,
the rock in his hand.
No! My curses on him!
You hear me, Cain?
I curse you back.

XIV

The rest is scattered and
cursed, Cain,
cracked against rocks
in your rage of last night.

Look at the moon.
Pale, shaped like an ear,
it hides in the clouds.

Take what I've gathered.
Go to the gate and tell the
angel
Abel deserves to sleep
inside of Eden.

XV

Fear?
I will tell you about fear,
Cain.
In the waste outside of Eden,
so close we could still see
and feel
the annihilating glory of the
cherub's face,
we sank exhausted to our
knees in the dust:
Bone, brain, muscle, blood,
flesh
were one: ice.

At dawn,
wakened by the prod of the
sun,
I took your mother in my
arms and said,
"The cobra curves up
out of his nest,
and, with his narrow spine
and neck,
lifts his face to light.
He knows no God."

XVI

Come to my arms.
Lift your face…
Homicidal, venomous,
sprung from our loins,
he is still our son,
and we grieve.

But drink from the wine,
life will resume.
There will be others.

He has gone to the ends of
the earth
and his stabbing questions
have ceased.

XVII

Naked, I went from the
Maker,
where the animals mated
in the grass of the garden.

I stepped on the skulls
of the failed creations,
returned to the Father

with a hand on my snake,
a corpse that was walking,
mocked at by angels.

It was a sickness of self,
a hunger for love,
ended by you.

I feel it again.

XVIII

So Cain has come back,
the prodigal king, Cain,
founder of cities,
commander of men
and the keeper of harems
for his sexual pleasure within
them,
whose gifts
are chaos and destruction.

You wrestled with Abel
in the womb of your mother
to emerge
covered with blood.
Why should you wonder
that I fight with your
mother?

XIX

Believe me, Cain,
this angel will take his blame
and blade
and rise, one day,
to the cold above the sun.

We will be dead,
and the garden empty,
but our bones will listen.

XX

He is tiny,
far thinner
than the one who slides
around the tree.

Squirming in my grasp,
he listens to the whispers
of the flaming sword
and gazes into the garden.

Cain,
he is my messenger,
moving back and forth
between my body
and the tree.

XXI

Knowing nothing and no one,
I awakened alone
and stood in the mist,
a creature of earth,
sluggish and wet.
'til the approach
of a voice and a wind,
penetrant breath—
I was possessed
chilled and embraced;
gust after gust,
thrilled my spine,
sweat poured from my flesh,
and I quaked
where I stood
in billowing fog
on the dark earth.
Full of ruffling blows,
coils and departures,
like questions and questions
and questions
and a testing caress,
as it dwindled and died.
"I am the Maker," it said.

XXII

What Do You Know?
An enigma to you, Cain,
who neither worship nor
love--
the Creator,
the Maker of Miracle
made me His likeness,
Mirror of Brightness!
And I exult
even in terror
at His approach.

After His presence,
knowledge and comfort
linger and linger.
I lie lightly, dreaming of
Eden,
restored to my state,
waking to hunger and
tremble,
and pray for His presence.

You, with your doubts and
derogations,
what do you know?

XXIII

You call it sin
to savor a fruit
Jehovah made sacred?

There was no sin
but yours, Cain,
the murder of Abel.

XXIV

Lord God, I stand before you
naked once again
in the loneliness I knew
before the birth of wife and
sons,
before your dread voice
called
and thrilled my marrow with
its call,
before the first wing-
thudding messenger
overshadowed me,
before I saw the snake's
seductive sway
and felt my thin blood ice,
I stand before you,
Unseen Lord,
most distant,
yet most intimate and dread,
and beg,
take me back.
Banish all the rest.
I will give you anything.

XXV

My God, Jehovah,
You said:
"Stretched up
beneath the cold white moon,
with mesmerizing eyes,
the snake awaits your going
out.

Or suns itself,
heavy,
upon the threshold
of your heart,
waiting
to be taken up
and brought inside."

From the moment
You forbade the fruit,
I yearned for it
and hated You
for setting it apart,
untouchable.

My sacrifice rejected,
I walked from the altar
far from my indulgent wife
and squabbling sons
to scream in silence
at the sky.

Cain in Exile

Graven on Cain's brow were scars that resembled a tree or a
man with many hands. When the flesh of his forehead moved,
the scars mimicked the lightning of summer storms. Often, as he
squatted in the fork of the stark tree surrounded by the moving
mist of morning, watching the villagers with his green hooded
eyes that seemed to droop with reptilian indifference, he fed on
the memory of his mark and the food it brought. For the villagers
feared him and would pile meat, skins of milk, cheese and fruit
on the roots of the tree as they ascended to the altar atop the
mountain. They assumed that whoever had marked him had also
turned his serpent hair white. With the thin nose and bloodless
lips of hunger, Cain would stare down at them. When the sun
dispelled the mist, he jumped down, ate, and left much for the
scavengers.

Those who came to retrieve what he left were careful to give
him time to stalk off into the dense grove to the left of the single,
central tree he squatted in. Once he grabbed a young child by the
ankles who had not seen him waiting in the rocks. Although Cain
had not harmed the boy, when he returned to his parents' hut he
said that Cain was like a snake that could swallow a man. This
was not the first time such an incident had occurred and when
the boy's father spread the story, there was talk of escorting the
stranger, without food, to the desert beyond the mountains.

However, the headman spoke in Cain's defense at the assembly.
He reminded his people that Cain helped at harvest time and would
accept no recompense. The ancient rose to his feet and the fire
gave him many beards as he said, "Are we to forget so easily what
the Gods have spoken through this man? The times he has sat in
front of the oven and praised the earth and her gifts? He has sung
of food as none of us can. In his eyes the wheat is immortal. He
speaks and the moon is forever full and still, and the stalks sigh
with desire to drop their grains into the hands of the children. And
the lovers think of pleasure in the fields. Or the moon waxes faster
than a woman great with child, and the heart of his hearer knows
that the ground waxes with food. In his speech praise of labor is
like unto the fulfilled promise of the labor. All of you heard him
the night he called the sickle moon the smile of night. He thanks

the ground when it wears the face of frost. Who can say that the ground or the Gods would not resent his death?"

Harvests passed. Early one evening when the new moon and the sun shared the horizon, and the frost was the face the ground wore, Cain descended the mountain and asked the headman for any one of his daughters. They discussed the gifts she would bring to her husband, and Cain left that same night with the girl and a bag of seeds. When his wife remonstrated with him, the headman answered, "He feels the other hunger."

Before Cain's appearances in the village had been unpredictable. He would appear in the midst of winter in what was obviously a dreadful hunger, sing the praises of the earth and refuse food. After the birth of his son, whatever darker powers and moods still possessed him he kept hidden from the sight of the villagers. His stories and songs began to sing human life in all of nature. He would not have it that only the spirits of the dead were in the world. "In the stark tree is the boy who is lean as the Bedouin. In a flowering pear tree is the girl he embraces. On the wheat stalks are the infants waiting patiently to be gathered home." He waxed eloquent and even foolish. The villagers often saw Cain play with the boy beneath the tree. He would catch him when he leapt from the fork. Together, they would swing from the branches. Above all, although the villagers never saw him in the act, Cain fed his son. Near the end of his wife's pregnancy, Cain had taken to sleeping alone. The terrible cries and mysterious words he uttered in his recurring nightmares had caused her to fear for the growing child. He would wake screaming that offal he ate was being taken from him. "I am sitting in the tree when the moon is blown from my sight by a bellowing voice. Lightning strikes the tree and I fall forever with the blasted wood surrounding and hitting me. When I hit the ground it is frozen and someone wrests food from me. One night it is myself, another you, another my mother or one of the boys I frightened." He glanced at the ground, then raised his face to his wife and spoke in a barely audible voice. "These dreams are worse than the ones that drove me into the village like a madman when I first came here. Perhaps you should return to the hut of your parents." His wife asked him if the crops had failed, and since he could not say yes, he resolved to endure the dreams and let her remain.

After the boy's birth, Cain slept soundly for a while, but as the boy grew the nightmares returned with an awful regularity. Now, those who stole his food were either his father, the headman or his brother, and when he pleaded with them their faces laughed and melted into his, as though a wax mask heated and reshaped itself by a demonic will that sprang from nowhere. This aspect of the dream blinded him with rage, and when his vision cleared he was a snake leaping from the fork of the tree to strike them.

In order to sleep in peace, he went to the village and sat in front of the oven and sang until he collapsed. He would sing long after the last of his audience went to sleep. On those nights he left the village and sang in the fields to the scorn and the smile of the moon. Yet he dreamed. As always he would accept no food as recompense from the villagers, but he started to accept drink brewed from the grain and finally, after drinking deeply, he was able to sleep. However, the brew impaired his songs, and the villagers began to mutter that Cain was waxing mad again as he had when first he came to the village. He vanished returning only to get brew from the headman. He practiced his songs alone in the mountains. When he returned, he found he still could not control his utterances. The grains he had planted in the clearing on the mountain were almost ripe and his wife spoke to him of the harvest. But for that he would have gone on drinking and singing before the oven.

For several days, he woke without memory. Then, a new nightmare visited him. He had harvested the grain, but his wife would appear holding a foul mess in her hands and ask if he expected her and the child to partake of it. She said, "So, this is the result of the magic of your praise. Who marked you should have cut out your tongue."

At twilight, Cain, with his son at his side, entered the clearing with a scythe. He worked furiously and the moon turned her face from the night and a mist obscured the stars and lay thick around him. Suddenly, he heard a voice issue from the tree and when he turned and gazed he noticed that the mist had lifted and a thick black serpent with a flickering tongue coiled in the fork of the tree. On its brow were marks similar to the ones on his forehead. He nodded slowly as the serpent spoke. "Get thee out of the headman's country, unto a land that I will show thee; and I will make of thee a great nation, and I will bless thee, and make thy name great; and thou shalt be a blessing; and I will bless them that bless thee, and curse him that curseth thee; and in thee shall all families of the earth be blessed. Look now toward heaven, and tell the stars, if thou be able to number them, so shall thy seed be. Behold, here I am. Take now thy son, thine only son, whom thou lovest, and get thee to the altar atop the mountain and offer him there for a burnt offering."

"I have never seen that snake before, Father," said Cain's son who had heard nothing. At the sound of the boy's voice, Cain wrenched round and stared hard at his son. Finally, he said, "Run home now and get two baskets and cord to bind the wheat."

When the boy returned, they ascended and Cain placed the baskets of wheat on the altar. He kindled a fire and when it caught he called his son. As the flames set the wheat ablaze, he grabbed the boy by the waist and ordered him to spread his arms. Raising the boy above the offering, Cain announced, "I will keep him."

Cain's Agon with God

I

There is this wound
Within and beneath my stomach
That no one will ever make naked:
A scar, a mouth,
Howl of my soul,
Father, mother, and brother.
When my manhood lifts,
I wish I had never been born.

II

You think so?
I, his keeper?
You,
Lord of the World,
You could not keep him,
So, now that I've struck
You assign him to me.
Thoughtful of you.

III

As Adam's fists,
Which battered my face,
Shook my thighs,
Buckled my knees,
And sprawled me in the dust
Were meant to drive
Satan out of me,
So I intended the rock
With which I bashed my brother's brow
To expel
The pious love of You.

IV

You Who create
With a word, a thought or a breath,
Who was the first
To shudder with bliss
Or grovel before You?
There must have been many,
Not only Adam,
That wretched descendant.
The tree You forbid us
Grows from the grave
Of the former creations
Buried beneath it
To feed its roots!
There should be candles in skulls
In a circle around it.

V

Why do You hunger
For the gifts of the dust?
Fruits, grains, beasts
Can mean nothing to You,
Immortal God,
You who walk in cool evening
To eat of the fruit
Forbidden to us,
Why should you care for the savor
Of farmgifts and huntflesh,
Smoke of holocausts
Rising, surging
Over the altar,
Filling your nostrils?
You Who inhabit
The thinness of wind
And move from the heights
Beyond the moon and stars
The eye cannot reach
To rush to the Earth
More quick than the Eagle,
Who coil like a snake
Immense as the world
Or gently as Father
Caressing Eve's flesh,
Why do You hunger
For the gifts of the dust?

VI

The baskets of fruit
And the sheaves of the wheat
Were abundant and fine,
Glowing and ripe,
Heaped on the altar
In the hope they might please,
But You flung up a wind,
Scattered my gifts
In the dust
And pronounced them unfit,
Astonishing Adam, Abel and Eve,
Who backed from my presence
As from a serpent
Or midden of shit,
Muttering prayers.

Now they are planning my exile.
Adam and Abel announced it,
And I am less than a goat
Packed with their sins
To be chased through the gates
To die by hunter or hunger.
Rejecting, jealous God,
Tempter and tormentor,
Yes, I am a sinner.

Yes, violent of temper.
An eager asker of fractious questions,
Half crazy with lust
And the need to be loved,
Afraid of father, brother and mother,
And full of murderous urges.
I do not deny it.

But You are a judge
Without mercy.

VII

I bent my head to the water.
I saw Your burning signature,
The whiteness of my serpent locks,
My hollow cheeks and haunted eyes.
My reflection crawled and shuddered,
Writhed and broke.

Ague shook my bones.

VIII

Open, raw,
Aflame on my brow,
Your mark of bloody ownership,
A brazen and reflecting shield,
Rejecting pity and contempt.
Spare me your protection.
Erase the burning brand.
Make smooth my goug'd brow,
Signature and punishment
Too great to bear.

IX

Let me remain
A scapegoat among them.
A villain and curse.
"Snake!"
Yes, it is better
To tremble and stutter,
In impotent rage,
Torment their dreams,
Than wander alone
Hounded by fears.

X

What should I do?
Get down on my knees
To breathe into his nose,
Empty my lungs into his nostrils,
And bring him to life
As You did Adam,
Favored by You?

If You love him so much,
Do it Yourself.

XI

Will I truly be safe, Yahweh,
With scars on my brow,
Staff in my hand,
And a dog at my side
To fight off curs
Who snarl at my coming?
Will my exile end
In heartfelt repentance
For the death of Abel, the faithful?
Will I walk, then, forgiven,
Across the fields of my father,
Without fear of my brothers?

XII

"Cain with his questions,
His frenzy,
His fears,
Jealous, impious Cain,
Cain, who clings to the skirts
Of his mother,
Afraid of my wrath,
Whining, cowering Cain…"
Over and over and over
And You wonder at murder?

XIII

Should I pound at my head
With a rock?
I weep and repent.
Enough!

XIV

He shrugged,
Then listened, looking away.
When I demanded an answer,
He suggested I search
In my sins
Where I surely would find
Something offensive to God,
If not to myself.
That's when I struck,
Again and again,
Crying, "Search in these blows,
O Favorite of God.
Now, anguished I struggle
To feel compassion for him
Burdened by favor,
For myself,
With a mark on my brow.

XV

The inexplicable words
Stinging my face
Like a slap of dismissal
Before I had knowledge
Forbidden and evil,
Rooted and grew within,
Gripping the soil of the heart
With unquenchable thirst,
Uprooted its ground,
The home of my nature,
A serpent that lurked at the threshold,
Risen to strike.

Cain to Abel

I.

At first,
There was one,
Adam, the Master,
Unrivalled.
Now,
There are brothers
Who envy their father,
But tremble to show it.
Is it not so,
Abel, my brother,
You, whose face I see
When I look for my own
In the still waters of dream?

II

I would do anything
To quiet the voice
That argues within.
The unceasing voice
That drives me to fight
With arrogant Adam—
That tyrant!
And rages and quails
At the peacekeeping gestures and words
Of smooth, solicitous Eve!

O, brother, blest is your peace!

III

Scream to the sky.
Call on your God
To raise you from death.
Perhaps He is sleeping
Having fed on the savor
Of smoke that rose
From the goat you butchered
And left for His hunger,
Caressing, then slitting his throat,
Solemn,
After glancing at me.
Lie dead on the ground,
Pious and pure,
Possessor of sensuous, red lips,
No longer laughing and mocking,
Betrayer of secrets,
Who would not be silent.
Provoke me no longer,
Flesh of my father and mother.

IV

The others have gone.
Abel lies here,
Here, in the field
Where I lured him
And struck till he fell.
Sudden and swift,
The thought and the blow.
His eyes wide
To the dome of the sky,
As the stone flashed
Toward his head.
Innocent Abel,
Who could not conceive
The depth of my hate
And laughed at my warnings.
O, I had heard it within,
That canker that whispered,
Or roared and shaped its intent.
I knew that it lurked,
Patiently gnawing, urging.

"Brother, your cries have been heard,
And I am punished to the bounds of endurance.
My exile is near.
The agon with Yahweh
Over and lost.
His mark on my brow,
I shake like leaves
In icy winds,
And I envy you still."

Cain to Adam

I

I want to be like my father
At the start of creation,
Like you, Adam,
Near to the Maker:
Ecstatic!
Dreaming of love
And the sons I will make:
Unfallen.

II

Tell me again that myth of my childhood:
How, when you were lonely
And stared at the beasts,
God, in His mercy, took pity
And spoke.
Silver and golden,
In the shape of a snake,
As long as a man
And fluid as water,
He circled the tree:
Flashes of lightning
Leaped in the leaves:
He denied you the apple
You always had eaten
And promised you Eve.

III

I witness the violence
Between you,
And hear how you curse,
Wishing for death
In your terror of God,
Who never appears.
Truth?
What is your truth?
That a serpent
Slept with my mother?
That Satan appears
As a virgin to tempt you?
That I am a snake
Fathered by him
To torment you?

IV

Shaking and naked,
I lay tied to the altar,
Unable to plead,
As you lifted the blade.

Why did you spare me?
Was it to threaten
Again and again?
Or is it to please God?

V

Tell me, Father,
Here, at this altar,
Where gifts are accepted
Or not,
As Jehovah sees fit,
Now that I know
How the meanings of prayers
Fork from the heart,
How does it feel
To creep in spirit
Like a worm
When you could halt
At the top of the steps,
Stand unprotected,
And ask for a reason,
Godlike,
Undaunted by death?

VI.

As fallen as you from the heights of the Godhead,
From power, exemption from death,
Conjoining with Eve in connubial bliss,
Possessing the Garden in a garment of light,
Prophetic and prescient, knowing the might of Jehovah
          and angels
In the mists of the future,
And vouchsafed visions of heaven,
As fallen as you, extinguished and hungry,
Unknowing, consumed and disgusted by sex,
With soot in my soul, banished to sweat in a wasteland,
As fallen as you,
Forgetting or cursing transcendence,
I would have murdered my wife and myself.
Yet you survive in bitterness in endurance,
And I am a killer, the joy of my soul slaughtered by you.

VII

Who says?
God!
God says
You pious hypocrite.
His mark upon my brow,
I am protected from your touch,
Inviolate.
Back off!
Sign of a sinner?
Think, fool.
Perhaps I am preserved
To kill again.

VIII

I will return to Mac Pelah,
The foretold place of sacred graves
Where the scent of Eden's orchards
Is consolation on the breeze.
From the tumult of towering cities,
Where I will reign a mighty king,
With the scars of God's approval,
I will return to Mac Pelah
To ask you to forgive me, Father,
When you lie down to die.

Cain and Aklia

I

Cain: You are afraid?
   My father is dying.
Aklia: Do as you like,
   I release you.
   Be loyal to them both,
   your mother and father.
   Do it.
   I, too, will be loyal.
Cain: Though rage pounds in my heart,
   it is time to return.

Cain, Alone

I

O, yes, I will offer
The best of my harvest
To Jehovah, the Knower Almighty,
Maker of evil and weakness,
The setter of snares,
And the green paths
Of the trap.
The maze He inhabits,
Where the wind of His spirit
Slides like a snake
In the air that we breathe,
Prison and wasteland
Laden with flowers
Adam and Hevah
Mistake for a bower
And slave to maintain.

II

With threats, sneers,
And his hand's wave,
I was dismissed
From the table of gifts,
Feast of their harvest,
By a master of slaves,
Traitorous brother,
And spellbinding witch—
That I must bear,
Beaten, reviled—
Her wedded grief
And curs'd secret—
Fawning caress, lingering look,
Seductive demand
I swallow rage
Squirming to burst,
Ready to leap
Like a snake
From my throat.
Her favors and looks
Kindled his wrath
To harp and harass,
Pursue like a hound,
Nip, leap, bite,
Rend, feast!
Now, afraid of their God,
Burdened by murder
And blasphemous rage,
I go like a goat—
O, to bash them with rocks,
Tyrant, brother, witch...

III

I dreamed of their words,
More naked than flesh,

Of the leaves
Shaped like their hearts,

Of their hearts
Bitten like apples.

IV

Let it be Adam entered in
His garden-wife with flaming rod,
Tiller of lands with sweat and grin,
Who banished me as far as Nod.
I have returned despite his God,
And naked to the eyes of Eve,
I'll kill the snakes that crawl this sod.
In ordained death all men believe.

Let it be me when sane or mad—
I hate myself with whose own will?
I've heard them wail for what they had,
And still they weep for what they swill.
My thirst for blood is with me still,
Though I enjoy their God's reprieve.
Abel lived to pray, to tend, to kill.
In ordained death all men believe.

Let it be God Himself, Who grew
The gifts that I and Abel brought,
Who, powerful in what He knew,
Cast me forth when I was caught,
Against great guilt I've lived and sought—
Oh, cunning God, to coil, deceive
With subtle wrath the works you wrought.
In ordained death all men believe.

Angel, with your flaming sword,
You guard an entrance to the grave,
But Adam's skull is your reward,
And gardens are too desolate to save.

V

You rose from the mud,
Where you lay like a worm,
To bite at the brow
Of Abel your brother,
Spilling his blood,
As though it was poison.
Now the voices inside
Are hissing the names
Of your father and mother.

VI

To hear Abel's voice
I discarded my crown,
Cast off the coils of my wealth,
The unbearable weight of my robe,
And knelt in the dirt.

It whispered,
And, sobbing, I rubbed at my scars
with the dust of the grave.

VII

I was terrified to die
By the bite of a serpent.
But now,
I have been hunting
In the long shadows of dawn,
Up and down the hills,
Overturning rocks,
Disturbing the gardens of little gods
Who crawl along the earth and lie,
As limp as both my parents,
Just beyond the bounds of Eden.

VIII

"Brother," he laughed,
Extending the knife,
You look so angry,
Your complexion is black.
Forgive me my favor.
You kill the sheep.
Beg Jehovah's forgiveness
And perform the slaughter.
What does it matter
Who cuts the throat
Of the wooly four legs
Given to God, as long
As savory odors rise
To the place where he hovers,
Eager to sniff billows of smoke,
And sated, then slumber
Like a beast in the winter,
Deafer and dumber
Than the rocks of this altar.
Perhaps he will sleep on the ground,
Taking on flesh,
And lie in the dust
In the skin of a serpent,
Whose head we can crush
Before we sit down together
And feast on this meat."
So Abel spoke, seeing my basket

Ignored and hearing Jehovah's reproach.
And I thought, Why please the Lord?
If He loves my brother so much,
Give Him the brain, the bowels,
The heart, and the member,
And I chuckled so darkly,
Abel flinched at my laughter.

IX

Screaming for vengeance,
I dug up the grave
And scattered his bones,
Flung them with curses,
And hammered his skull
At a rock until the stone broke:

I shuddered and woke.

Cain to Eve

I

You ask me how I've been?
The hairs upon my head stand up.
They yank upright
With silent, opened mouths,
And I stand rooted to the drenching earth
Beneath the close, mild moon,
Wishing I could fly
And that my face
Could strike God dead.

II

I knew you'd shrink away in shock, and shake
To see me standing in the door
Blocking the beams of the blood-red, setting sun,
casting shadow on your sheltered lap.
Return to the braiding of your hair—
So little goes on to its end with pleasure
Anymore, or should I say ever since
We saw the doubleness of all we do:
How assertion of ourselves denies our God
His creatures' love which once was pure and true.
Stay where you are. The darkness may conceal
Whatever weapon you'd be reaching for.
A weighty one most likely, one heavy
Enough to bash my brow and get a skull
For God, a meaty and permitted fruit

Since power, vengeance and possession
Are His and only holy His alone,
But I have tested that and lived despite
The horror of my punishment, His unwanted
Mark upon my brow and forgiving love.
Because I tower over you, you will not look
Directly in my face. Your wide and deep
Blue eyes avoid my snaky hair
Haloed by the weary, falling sun.
I seem so often like a tree,
A tree whose branches stretch like snakes,
Angry, wind exultant snakes.

In dreams, I see two snaky trees embrace.
I'll yank you to your feet to meet my face.
Bitch, your spit is better fit for God Almighty's eyes.
I give no good God damn. I've come to find
Out where the corpse of Abel has been buried
Because I plan to dig him up and take
His grimy, fractured skull up to the gate
And thrust it like an apple up into the cherub's sight,
A gift to the God who made us all
And offer it for hanging on
The tree He has forbidden us.

III

The wine sack lay beyond his arm.
My eyes fingered the distance
To the limp, pale snake,
The subtle serpent, Satan,
The mythic monster,
Enemy of God.
I put my hand upon my own thick beast,
And looked upon your husband
In his sleep.

IV

A terrible thought
Entered your heart,
Dear Mother,
And rose like a snake
Seduced by the moon:
Eating the fruit
Was like eating God,
And if you succeeded,
God surely would die.
You whispered to Adam
When he lay in your arms,
Drowsing and sated,
And then you discovered
The hunger he'd hidden.

V

Awakened again,
You stared at the serpent
Shrunk on the thigh of your lover.
It puzzled your hunger.
You saw you were second,
Less perfect than Adam
And other. That was the riddle
That puzzled your love,
Especially naked.

VI

I dreamed I slid among the clothes,
Wrapped myself
Around her waist,
And said,
"Forget the fire,
Tongs and roasting meat.
Caress my brow
And narrow neck.

Until Cain comes."

VII

Like to the Father?"
With eyes that are open?"
Could you not reply
"Why should I eat
What is forbidden
When I eat with my Maker each day?"
Did you say that
Or even think it in silence?
No, you looked at the snake
And thought, "How God-like it is,
And human."

VIII

Collapsed on the glowing, sunset grass,
You saw the maw of night's shadow
Glide swift as a snake,
Like a tide of black water
Under the cold, blank, round of the moon
And shivered and turned
To look at the angel
And saw the gesture he made,
The blaze of his blade...

Then the consoler in Heaven,
The Giver of Exile,
Added fire to the gifts He had given.

Return

I

You see, wife,
I have returned
Your son at my side,
Unharmed as I promised.
He has knelt in their tent,
And received blessing,
Mixed as it was
With remembrance and warning.
He understands his nature,
Connected to God the Creator,
By the encounter with Adam and Eve,
First of the human.
Now when he kills,
It won't be his father.

II

At dusk, at the edge of the fields,
We sat watching the fire,
Meat roasting on a spit,
Inhaling the smell,
After the back-warping work of the day.
Glowing from labor,
Watching fireflies and stars,
We drank wine,
And Adam softened,
Turned when he spoke,
And looked at my face,
Forgot his complaints,
Dropped his demands,
Smiled,
And I blent with his nature,
Like smoke with the sky.